BETTE MIDLER
GREATEST HITS
EXPERIENCE THE DIVINE

EDITOR
Carol Cuellar

BOOK DESIGN
Richard Chimelis

PHOTOGRAPHY
Greg Gorman

COVER ART
© 1993 Atlantic Recording Corporation in the U.S.
and WEA International Inc. outside the U.S.

Copyright © 1993 CPP/Belwin, Inc.
15800 N.W. 48th Avenue, Miami, FL 33014
International Copyright Secured   Made In U.S.A.   All Rights Reserved

CONTENTS

(From the Film "THE ROSE")

THE ROSE

Words and Music by
AMANDA McBROOM

Slowly ♩ = 66

Some say love it is a riv-er that drowns the ten-der reed. Some say

love it is a ra-zor that leaves your soul to bleed. Some say love it is a hun-ger an end-less ach-ing

need. I say love it is a flow-er and you its on-ly

THE WIND BENEATH MY WINGS

Words and Music by
LARRY HENLEY and JEFF SILBAR

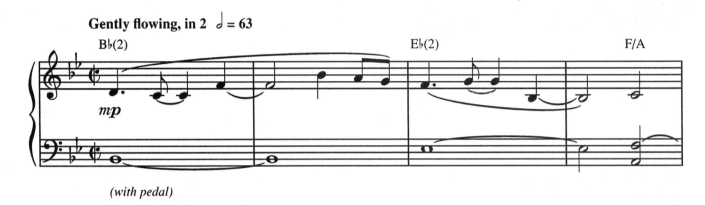

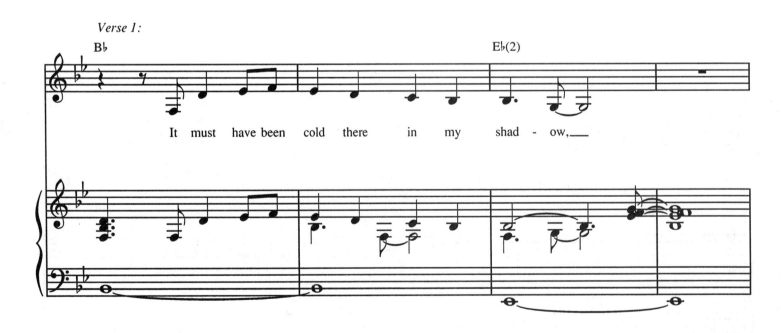

It must have been cold there in my shad - ow,___

The Wind beneath My Wings - 6 - 1

to nev - er have sun - light on your face.

You were con - tent to let___ me_____ shine, that's your way,___

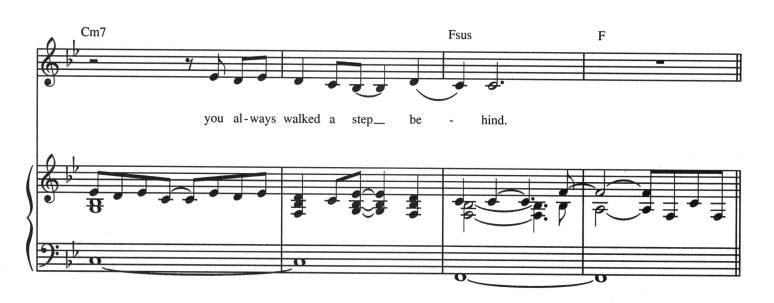

you al - ways walked a step__ be - hind.

8

So, I___ was the one with all___ the glo - ry,
It might_ have ap - peared to go___ un - no - ticed,

while you__ were the one with all___ the strength.
but I've__ got it all here in___ my heart.

A beau - ti - ful face with-out_ a name___ for so long,_
I want you to know I know_ the truth,___ of course I know_ it,

a beau - ti - ful smile to hide__ the pain.
I___ would be noth - ing with - out you.

cresc.

FRIENDS

By
BUZZY LINDHARDT
and MARK KLINGMAN

DO YOU WANT TO DANCE?

By
ROBERT FREEMAN

BOOGIE WOOGIE BUGLE BOY

Words and Music by
DON RAYE and HUGHIE PRINCE

Brightly, with a swing ♩ = 192

3-part harmony:

He was a fa-mous trum-pet man out Chi-ca-go way;— he
(2nd time inst. solo ad lib. . . .

had a boo-gie style that no one else could play.— He was the top man of his craft,—

Boogie Woogie Bugle Boy - 6 - 1

FROM A DISTANCE

Lyrics and Music by
JULIE GOLD

Slowly ♩ = 66

Verse:

1. From a dis-tance, the world looks blue and green, and the snow-capped mountains white. From a dis-tance, the o-cean meets the stream, and the ea-gle takes to

From a Distance - 4 - 1

Verse 2:
From a distance, we all have enough,
And no one is in need.
There are no guns, no bombs, no diseases,
No hungry mouths to feed.
From a distance, we are instruments
Marching in a common band;
Playing songs of hope, playing songs of peace,
They're the songs of every man.
(To Bridge:)

Verse 3:
From a distance, you look like my friend
Even though we are at war.
From a distance I just cannot comprehend
What all this fighting is for.
From a distance there is harmony
And it echos through the land.
It's the hope of hopes, it's the love of loves.
It's the heart of every man.

HELLO IN THERE

By
JOHN PRINE

Moderately slow ♩ = 63

1. We had an a - part - ment   in the
2. Me and my hus - band,   we don't
3. So   if you're walk - ing   down the

cit - y,   me and   my hus-band   liked_
talk much an - y - more._   He sits   and stares   through_
street some - time,   and you should spot some   hol -

Hello in There - 4 - 1

MISS OTIS REGRETS
(She's Unable to Lunch Today)

Words and Music by
COLE PORTER

ONE FOR MY BABY
(And One More for the Road)

Lyric by
JOHNNY MERCER

Music by
HAROLD ARLEN

Slowly and freely

SHIVER ME TIMBERS

Words and Music by
TOM WAITS

swal-low me, don't fol-low me; I'm trav-'ling a-lone.___ Blue

wa-ter's my daugh-ter; I skip like a stone.___

And the

Verse 2:
And I know Joe Conrad will be proud of me;
Many more before me've been called by the sea.
To be up in the crow's nest, singin' my saying:
Shiver me timbers, let's all sail away.
(To Bridge:)

Verse 3:
Won't you please call my family; tell them not to cry;
My goodbyes are written by the moon in the sky.
Say hey, nobody knows me; I got no reason to stay.
Shiver me timbers, I'm sailin' away.
(To Coda)

WHEN A MAN LOVES A WOMAN

Words and Music by
CALVIN LEWIS and ANDREW WRIGHT

When a Man Loves a Woman - 5 - 1

When a Man Loves a Woman - 5 - 2

ONLY IN MIAMI

By
MAX GRONENTHAL

1. Walk - ing a - long the beach last night,

Standing on the shore-line wait-ing,
ev-'ry-one an-ti-ci-pat-ing, I can hear the bro-ken-heart-ed
say: On-ly in Mi - am - i____ is Cu-ba__ so
far____ a-way.____

IN MY LIFE

Words and Music by
JOHN LENNON and PAUL McCARTNEY

CHAPEL OF LOVE

By
PHIL SPECTOR, ELLIE GREENWICH
and JEFF BARRY

Spring is here, and the sky is so ver-y blue.
Bells will ring, and the sun is gon - na shine.

Birds all sing, as if they knew,
I'm gon - na be his, he's gon - na be mine.

to - day's the day we'll say "I do." And we'll
We're gon - na love un - til the end of time. And we'll

Chapel of Love - 3 - 1

Chorus:

never be lonely anymore.___ 'Cause we're

go - in' to the chap - el, and we're gon - na get mar - ried.

Go - in' to the chap - el and we're gon - na get mar - ried.

Gee,___ I real - ly love you, and we're gon - na get mar - ried.

EXPERIENCE THE DIVINE